Lisbon is fast evolving into a c......
talents making great use of lo......
innovative food, art, shopping ......
the city has emerged as an ene......
where street murals and histor......
a plethora of inventive ideas. So...... ......
doesn't boast the glitz of many ......pean capitals. Instead the
raw, authentic charm of this coastal city has worked wonders in
enchanting visitors and inspiring residents.

CITIx60: Lisbon explores the Portuguese capital in five aspects,
covering architecture, art spaces, shops and markets, eating and
entertainment. With expert advice from 60 stars of the city's creative scene, this book guides you to the real attractions of the city for
an authentic taste of Lisbon life.

Contents

Before You Go

BASIC INFO

Currency
Euro (EUR/S)
Exchange rate: €1 : $1.1

Time zone
GMT +1
DST +2

DST begins at 0100 (local time) on the last
Sunday of March and ends at 0300 (local time)
on the last Sunday of October.

Dialling
International calling: +351
Citywide: 21

Weather (avg. temperature range)
Spring (Mar-May): 14-18°C / 57-64°F
Summer (Jun-Sep): 20-28°C / 68-82°F
Autumn (Oct-Nov): 14-19°C / 57-66°F
Winter (Dec-Feb): 8-12°C / 47-54°F

USEFUL WEBSITES

Bus & tram journey planner
carris.transporteslisboa.pt

Metro map & ticket info
www.metrolisboa.pt

EMERGENCY CALLS

Ambulance, fire or police
112

Non-emergency police
+351 213 421 634

Embassies
China   +351 213 928 430
Germany   +351 218 810 210
Spain   +351 291 703 310
France   +351 213 939 100
UK   +351 808 203 537
US   +351 291 235 636

AIRPORT EXPRESS TRANSFER

Lisbon Airport <-> Saldanha (Metro Red Line)
Trains / Journey: every 6-9 mins / 20 mins
From Airport or Saldanha: 0630-0100 daily
One-way: €1.45
www.metrolisboa.pt

Lisbon Airport <-> Cais do Sodré (Aerobus 1)
Buses / Journey: every 20-25 mins / 40 mins
From Airport & Cais do Sodré: 0800-2300 daily
24hr Aerobus Pass: €3.15 / Return: €4.95
www.aerobus.pt

PUBLIC TRANSPORT IN LISBON

Metro
Bus
Ferry
Train
Tram (Carris)
Taxi

Means of Payment
Lisboa Card*
Viva Viagem Card
Credit cards
Cash

*Card can be purchased for 1-3 days use.

PUBLIC HOLIDAYS

January	1 New Year's Day
March/April	Good Friday, 25 Freedom Day
May	1 Labour Day, Corpus Christi
June	10 Portugal Day, 13 Feast of St. Anthony
August	15 Assumption Day
October	5 Republic Day
November	1 All Saints Day
December	1 Independence Day, 8 Immaculate Conception, 25 Christmas Day

Galleries and museums are likely to be closed on
Mondays and around Christmas and new year's
day. Smaller shops may close on public holidays.

FESTIVALS / EVENTS

March
ModaLisboa (also in October)
modalisboa.pt
EDP Lisbon Half Marathon
www.running-portugal.com/lisbon/lisbonhalf/
en/registration
Lisboa Na Rua (through April)
lisboanarua.com

April
Lisbon Fish & Flavours
www.peixemlisboa.com

May
IndieLisboa
indielisboa.com
Alkantara Festival (biennial, through June)
www.alkantarafestival.pt
Out Jazz (through September)
FB: Out Jazz
ARCOlisbon
www.ifema.es/arcolisboa_06/

June
Feira do Livro de Lisboa
feiradolivrodelisboa.pt
Festas de Lisboa
www.festasdelisboa.com
Arraial Pride
www.ilga-portugal.pt/lisboapride

July
NOS Alive
nosalive.com

September
Caixa Alfama
www.caixaalfama.pt
Outfest
www.outfest.pt

October
DocLisboa
www.doclisboa.org

Event days vary by year. Please check for
updates online.

UNUSUAL OUTINGS

Underdogs Public Art Tour
www.under-dogs.net/public-art/

Muraliza Mural Art Festival
FB: muralizacascais

We Hate Tourism Tours
www.wehatetourismtours.com

Epic Surf School
www.epicsurfschool.pt

The Best Portugal Wine Stories & Tours
www.thebestportugal.com

SMARTPHONE APP

Bike routes planning & navigation
Lisboa Horizontal (iOS only)

Real-time Metro service updates
Lisbon Metro (iOS only)

Public transport journey planner
Lisboa MOVE-ME

Tide predictions for surfers
Magic Seaweed

REGULAR EXPENSES

Domestic letters / international airmail
€0.47 / €0.75-0.80

Viva Viagem Carris/Metro (single ticket)
€0.50+1.45

Gratuities
Diners: 10% for waitstaff & bartenders
Hotels: €1@bag for the porter, €1 daily for
cleaners
Licensed taxis: 5-10%

Count to 10

What makes Lisbon so special?

Illustrations by Guillaume Kashima aka Funny Fun

Lisbon's rich heritage and traditions are the foundations for the city's forward-thinking culture and buzzing creativity. From legendary markets and religious monuments to contemporary galleries and haute cuisine, Lisbon champions its history whilst looking keenly to the future. Whether you are on a one-day stopover or a week-long stay, see what Lisbon creatives consider essential to see, taste, read and take home on your trip.

BEM VINDO A LISBOA!!!

MAAT LISBON

1

Architecture

Pavilhão de Portugal
by Alvaro Siza Vieira

Pavilhão do Conhecimento
by João Luís Carrilho da Graça

Centro Champalimaud (#3)
by Charles Correa Associates

Gare do Oriente Station
by Santiago Calatrava

EDP Headquarters (#1)
by Aires Mateus Architects

Fundação Calouste Gulbenkian (#12)
*by Alberto Pessoa, Pedro Cid &
Ruy Jervis d'Athouguia*

Casa das Historias Paula Rego
by Eduardo Souto de Moura

**Museu de Arte, Arquitetura e
Tecnologia (MAAT)**
by AL_A

Dimensional Fado Experience

Museu do Fado
Fado history & guitar workshop
www.museudofado.pt

NOS Alive
The only music festival with
a fado stage
www.nosalive.com

Fado in Chiado
50-mins performances in theatre
www.fadoinchiado.com

Sr. Vinho
Owned by top performer Maria da Fé
& features an all-star line up
R. Meio à Lapa 18, 1200-724

Povo
Savory petiscos & resident fadistas
www.povolisboa.com

Sr. Fado de Alfama
Cosy spot for street fado
R. dos Remédios 176, 1100

Signature Memento

Modern handmade footwear
Eureka Shoes
www.eurekashoes.com

Azulejo (Portuguese glazed tiles)
Cortiço & Netos (#25),
d'Orey Azulejos, *www.doreytiles.pt*

Ceramic art & tableware
Bordallo Pinheiro
bordallopinheiro.com

Homeware, body care & stationery
A Vida Portuguesa (#34)
www.avidaportuguesa.com

Canned fish
Conserveira de Lisboa
www.conserveiradelisboa.pt

Pastries

Califa
Assorted cakes
www.califa.com.pt

Pastéis de Belém
Pastel de nata (Custard tart)
www.pasteisdebelem.pt

A Padaria Portuguesa
Pão de deus
(Brioche with coconut topping)
www.apadariaportuguesa.pt

Choco & Mousse
Torrada (Double layer
butter-filled toast)
FB: @chocomousse.delicias

Pastelaria Careca
Palmiers, *pastelariaocareca.pt*

Fabrica Lisboa
Croissants
www.fabricalisboa.com

5

Classic Dishes

Bacalhau a bras (Stir-fry codfish)
Any restaurant

Grilled sardines
A Toscana
www.toscanacasadepasto.com

Tuna in sesame
Taberna da Rua das Flores (#46)
FB: A Taberna da Rua das Flores

Swordfish
Atira-te ao Rio
www.atirateaorio.pt

Tremoços (Lupin beans)
Any bar

6

Local Wine & Beer

Ginjinha
Ginginha do Carmo
FB: @ginginhadocarmo

**Port Wine, Vinho Verde
& Licor Beirão**
Garrafeira Nacional
www.garrafeiranacional.com

Sovina
www.sovina.pt

Dois Corvos Craft Brewery
www.doiscorvos.pt

Oitava Colina
www.oitavacolina.pt

7

Privileged Vantage Points of Lisbon

**Quiosque do Miradouro de São
Pedro de Alcântara**
FB: @SPedroAlcantara

Quiosque da Ribeira das Naus
FB: @RibeiradasNausLisboa

Quiosque Portas do Sol
Lgo. Portas do Sol, 1100-411

BANANACAFE
FB: @BANANACAFE.LISBOA

**Quiosque O Melhor Bolo de
Chocolate do Mundo**
FB: @QuiosqueOMelhorBolode-
ChocolatedoMundo

**Biblioteca Quiosque Jardim
da Estrela**
Jardim da Estrela, 1200-667

Quiosque Praça de São Roque
Lgo. Trindade Coelho, 1200-470

8
Miradouro & more

Adamastor
View of Tagus River &
Ponte 25 de Abril bridge

Senhora do Monte
View of downtown Lisbon

Sophia de Mello Breyner / Graça
View of Lisbon valley

Castelo de S. Jorge
View of Lisbon valley

**Santo Estevão & Nossa Senhora
do Monte**
View of Tagus River

**Patio of Palace of Independência
@S.Domingos Square**
View of Baixa Pombalina & Castle Hill

**Roof @Igreja de São Vicente
de Fora (#10)**
View of Lisbon valley

9
Seasonal activities

**Caracóis (snails with garlic
& oregano)**
Enjoy them outdoor with a cold
beer in summer

Jacaranda tree blossoms
Watch they turn the city purple in
late spring (lasts two weeks)

Festas da Lisboa street parties
Enjoy grilled sardines & traditional
music at street corners

Hitting the beach
Take advantage of the city's
proximity to natural beaches in
the summer

**Free live music shows in
city parks**
Try Out Jazz & Lisboa Na Rua held
between Spring & Autumn

10
Leisurely Routes

**Ride a bike along path
Belém–Cais do Sodré**
Designed by P-06 atelier (p.052) &
runs along Tagus River

Ride the Cacilheiro ferry
Runs from Cais do Sodré pier to
Cacilhas

**Hop on & off the vintage
wooden Tram 28**
Head to Campo de Ourique

**Cruise Bica, Alfama & Castelo
on foot**
Visit squares and alleys of the
domestic districts

Explore Campo de Ourique
Visit celebrity graveyard &
Fernando Pessoa museum

Visit Sintra (#8) & Cascais
Scenery of neighbouring towns

Icon Index

🕐	Opening hours	💲	Admission
🏠	Address	f	Facebook
📞	Contact	URL	Website
📎	Remarks		

 Scan QR codes to access Google Maps and discover the area around each destination. Internet connection required.

60x60

60 Local Creatives x 60 Hotspots

From vast cityscapes to the tiniest glimpses of everyday exchange, there is much to provoke one's imagination. 60x60 points you to 60 haunts where 60 arbiters of taste develop their good taste.

Landmarks & Architecture

SPOTS · 01 – 12

Discover the breathtaking remains that survived the 1755 earthquake and marvel at the modern structures interspersed amongst the city's breathtaking skyline.

Cultural & Art Spaces

SPOTS · 13 – 24

Visit the bigger museums and collections for a peek into an influential art history. Small independent galleries offer a portal into Lisbon's pioneering art scene.

Markets & Shops

SPOTS · 25 – 36

Explore the boutiques that preserve Portuguese craftsmanship, haggle through the many markets selling fresh produce and scour through the designer outlets for a unique buy.

Restaurants & Cafés

SPOTS · 37 – 48

Lisbon's booming culinary culture embraces international influences whilst remaining loyal to its roots. Expect everything from glossy Japanese fusion to seafood sharing platters.

Nightlife

SPOTS · 49 – 60

The cobbled streets of Balto Alto and Cais do Sodré are filled with revellers throughout the early hours. Trail through these hotspots for trendy bars, premier clubs and warehouse parties.

Landmarks & Architecture

Contemporary structures, breathtaking ruins and panoramic city views

Lisbon's skyline is characterised by an endearing duality, where Gothic ruins and hidden pathways frame sleek modern buildings. Hit by a devastating earthquake in 1755, much of the city's pre-18th century architecture has been lost, although the breathtaking remains reveal a long history of Romanesque, Baroque, Renaissance and classical traditions. The capital's multilayered scenery can be seen high up from Panorâmico de Monsanto (#7), a compulsory visit for a grand 360-degree city view. Sintra's (#8) vast scenery is the perfect introduction to Lisbon's royal past, with Romantic and Neoclassical palaces set within lush greenery. Museu do Teatro Romano (#11) similarly provides a time capsule for a history dating back to the first century, housing an impressive theatre built during the Roman Empire. Whilst a visit to Museu Nacional do Azulejo (#4) offers a remarkable insight into the capital's decorative ceramic tile history.

Of course, Lisbon's modern additions provide a stunning contrast to the many well-preserved historical sites. The imposing 50-metre-tall concrete elevator (#2) was completed on the mark of the millennium and boasts unforgettable views of the Tagus. Centro Champalimaud (#3) is a scientific research institute that houses groundbreaking discoveries for cancer in a smooth-lined build marked by large circular windows and glass-panelled pathways. Another unsuspecting triumph is the contemporary design of the Energias de Portugal Headquarters (#1) – one of Europe's top electricity providers. Make time to visit Lisbon's most recent addition – MAAT (www.maat.pt) – and its extraordinary tile-covered structure that smoothly extends from the river-side promenade.

Matilde Travassos
Photographer

I'm Matilde. I work for fashion magazines like *Cosmopolitan*, but I also do personal work. I always thought I would live in New York, Paris, or London, but Lisbon is just perfect for me.

Elevador da Boca do Vento
P.015

Luis Borges
Model

A Portuguese model of high international success, Luís Borges has modelled for the likes of Dior Homme, Yves Saint Laurent and Hermès. His work has been duly recognised and awarded.

Rui Aguiar
Fashion photographer

Rui Aguiar shoots for major Portuguese fashion magazines and recently ModaLisboa.

EDP Headquarters
P.014

Centro Champali-maud
P.016

Frederico Duarte
Design writer & curator

I was born and bred in Lisbon but so far have lived in three continents. I'm a design writer and curator with an incurable case of wanderlust.

Praça do Comércio
P.022

Frederico Miranda
Founder, TODOS

Frederico Miranda is a film director at production company, Quioto. He also founded TODOS, a space for creatives to make and collaborate on visual content.

Sam Baron
Founder, Sam Baron and Co.

Sam Baron offers creative direction and design consultancy, embracing projects with a global approach where all creative skills blend to offer a challenging and original vision.

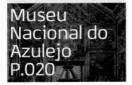

Museu Nacional do Azulejo
P.020

Panteão Nacional
P.023

Tamara Alves
Artist

I am no more than a girl who loves drawing. A rough passion and a primal instinct flow from my illustration, street art, and tattooing. The city and urban life are my inspiration.

Sintra
P.026

Mike El Nite
Artist, rapper, producer & DJ

I am Miguel Caixeiro. Born and raised in Lisbon, I love my city in all of its aspects and I feel that it loves me back. That's why I haven't left, even though it's hard to pay the bills as an artist.

Miguel Marcelino
Architect

Miguel Marcelino has worked in Switzerland and Spain before establishing his own office in Portugal. In 2014, he represented Portugal in the Venice Architecture Biennale.

Panorâmico de Monsanto
P.024

Convento da Ordem do Carmo
P.028

Ricardo Bak Gordon
Architect

Ricardo Bak Gordon works in many parts of the world, but from time to time, he reminisces his city and feels emotional when he returns to Lisbon.

Museu do Teatro Romano
P.030

Filipe Faísca
Fashion designer

Imagine a flying bird gliding, and now it rests on a roof. It focuses, realises, creates, receives and drives. Flies again. That's what I am.

Hélio Morais
Co-founder, HAUS

I'm also a part of Portuguese bands Linda Martini and PAUS. HAUS is a multidisciplinary space for recording, rehearsal, and a booking agency that puts music and brands together.

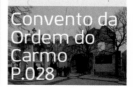

Igreja de São Vicente de Fora
P.029

Fundação Calouste Gulbenkian
P.031

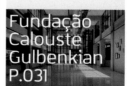

1 EDP Headquarters
Map B, P.106

Home to Energias de Portugal, one of Europe's top electricity providers, the EDP headquarters at the once-industrial riverfront was completed under the direction of Portuguese architects and brothers Manuel and Francisco Aires Mateus in 2015. To emphasise the sense of transparency and its connection to the city, sharp vertical blades wrap two office towers, connected by a low roof cascading over a public square. Go in broad daylight to experience the shadow play created by these beams. The many collaborations with big name architects, though many are still under way, are worthy of note.

🏠 *Av. 24 de Julho 12, 1249-300*
URL *www.edp.pt*

"Apart from being a work of art, the architecture brings to Lisbon a different perspective of future and a taste of contemporary cityscape."

– Matilde Travassos

2 Elevador da Boca do Vento

Map L, P.110

At 50 metres tall, this slimline concrete elevator provides an unlikely yet striking vantage point to view the city and its breathtaking coast. Erected in 2000 along the cliffs south of the Tagus River, the outdoor lift descends to former shipyard-turned-leisure area and park, alongside a variety of cafés and restaurants. Take a 15-minute ride on *cacilheiro* to cross the river and bask in the calming views. While on the south bank, Restaurante Atira-te ao rio or the grassy lawns on the waterfront are ideal for a leg-stretching break.

🕐 0800–0000 daily 💲 €1
🏠 Lgo. da Boca de Vento, 2800-034
🔗 10-minute Cacilheiro ride (every 7-35 minutes): from Cais do Sodré: 0535-0140 (M-F), 0540- (Sa-Su & P.H.), from Cacilhas: 0520-0120, €1.25, www.transtejo.pt

"This is simply mandatory for whoever is visiting Lisbon."

– Rui Aguiar

3 Centro Champalimaud
Map N, P.111

A state-of-the-art research centre and an architectural triumph famed for its futuristic accents, Champalimaud Centre for the Unknown is certainly out of this world. Aptly located where voyages to the "unknown" were made in the 1600s, the institute built by Indian architects Charles Correa Associates officially opened in 2010 to facilitate innovations for cancer and neuroscience. Linked by a 125-metre suspended glass tunnel, the two main buildings house colossal light-filled treatment rooms, laboratories and an auditorium lit by huge circular windows, fusing beauty with purpose. For those needing a rest, Darwin's Café on the waterfront is positioned to capture magnificent sunset views.

🏠 Av. Brasília, 1400-038
☎ +351 21 048 0200
URL www.fchampalimaud.org
🖉 Darwin's Café: 1230-1530, 1630-1830, 1930-2300 (Tu-Su), -1600 (M)

"The privileged view completes the design. The cylindric buildings are perfect for pictures."
– Luis Borges

4 Museu Nacional do Azulejo
Map M, P.111

Azulejos, the iconic ceramic tiles native to Portugal, are exhibited in their full glory at this museum housed within a stunning 16th-century convent. Although this elaborate hand-painted decor is all over the city, tiles of all sizes and styles and the rich history of this art can be found neatly chronicled across the multistorey monastic build. Prepare for an awe-struck encounter with a 23-metre mural depicting Lisbon's pre-earthquake coastal views made in 1738. Take time to trawl through the collections at this rather far off venue and admire the opulent St Anthony's Chapel before you go.

🕐 1000–1800 (Tu–Su)
💲 €5/free (monthly first Sundays)
🏠 R. da Madre de Deus 4, 1900–312
📞 +351 21 810 0340 URL www.museudoazulejo.pt

"A proper visit to the museum will take a whole morning or afternoon. Make sure to have lunch in the convent's winter garden."

– Frederico Duarte

5 Praça do Comércio

Map D, P.107

Formerly housing the royal palace up until the 1755 Great Lisbon earthquake, Commerce Square lined with gloriously yellow classical arcades is still popularly known as Palace Yard and brackets a 14-metre equestrian statue of King José I. Often referred to as the "Gateway to Lisbon", open views of the Tagus River backdrop the various yearly concerts and celebrations that enliven the area. For a relaxing afternoon, visit one of the many restaurants and cafés for a picturesque outdoor lunch, and be sure to visit the Lisboa Story Centre to learn about the city's past.

🏠 Pc. do Comércio, 1100-148
🔗 Lisboa Story Centre: 1000-2000 daily, €7/5/3, www.lisboastorycentre.pt

"Go for a morning run and take a break at the Columns Wharf, or enjoy the sunset here with a drink. You may want to check out the nearby Belas-Artes ULisboa too."

– Sam Baron, Sam Baron and Co.

6 Panteão Nacional
Map C, P.107

Starkly accenting the skyline of Alfama, Lisbon's oldest district, the 17th-century design was meant to be a church dedicated to Christian martyr Saint Engratia but never used as one. Since 1916, the spectacular Baroque construction has functioned as National Pantheon, enclosing the tombs of Portuguese presidents, political leaders and cultural figures within its multicoloured marble walls. Make your way to the large white dome added in 1966 to observe a breathtaking 360-degree view. From there, the Tagus River and city architecture can be seen to full effect.

🕐 Tu–Su: 1000–1700 (Oct–Mar), –1800 (Apr–Sep)
💲 €4/free (monthly first Sundays)
🏠 Campo de Santa Clara, 1100–471
📞 +351 21 885 4820 🌐 www.panteaonacional.pt
🔗 Feira da Ladra (Thieve's Market):
0600–1400 (Tu & Sa)

"Feira da Ladra nearby is a good place for shopping. Go to Focaccia in Giro or Santa Clara dos Cogumelos for lunch, or As Marias com Chocolate for dessert."
– Frederico Miranda, TODOS

7 Panorâmico de Monsanto
Map J, P.110

The glam of Lisbon life in the 1960s is still visible beneath the decrepit gables and gantries of Panorâmico de Monsanto. Set within Monsanto Forest Park, several hundred feet above sea level, the 7,000-square-metre modernist structure first took the guise of a restaurant in 1968 before its multiple reincarnations as a club, office space and bingo hall. Abandoned over ten years ago, the interior encloses a history intriguingly at odds with itself, where graffiti lives alongside detailed panels designed by ceramicist Querubim Lapa, and stunning period carpets dotted with rubble. Visit at dawn or dusk to view the city undisturbed.

 🏠 *Est. da Bela Vista, 1500–070*

"Enjoy the sunset. Don't wear flip flops – there is a lot of everything on the floor. Get ready to jump over a small fence."

– Tamara Alves

8 Sintra

Map O, P.111

Just north of Lisbon, this UNESCO World Heritage classified town oversees a cultural landscape that encompasses some of Europe's leading examples of Romantic, Neo-Manueline and Baroque architecture. Historical monuments of Portuguese royalty are couched within vast spans of forest and farmland, namely the National Palace of Sintra — Portugal's oldest royal residence, in addition to the 1,000-year-old Moorish Castle, the National Palace and Gardens of Queluz, and the Palace of Monserrate. If walking through this decadent landscape isn't enough, visitors can book a horse riding tour or a carriage ride through the stunning scenery.

🕐 💲 *Opening hours & admission vary with spots*
🕐 *+351 21 923 7300* 🔗 *www.parquesdesintra.pt*
🔗 *Parques of Sintra organises daily guided tours in the Palaces of Pena, Sintra and Queluz.*

"It's especially beautiful during the low season. If you're on a budget, just walk around the mountain and be amazed without entering a single monument."

– Mike El Nite aka Miguel Caixeiro

9 Convento da Ordem do Carmo
Map A, P.105

Characterised by Gothic detailing and famed for its medieval charm, Carmo Convent and Church may have fallen victim to the 1755 earthquake, but its ruins are still a wonder to marvel at. Constructed at the turn of the 14th century by the head of the Portuguese army, Nuno Álvares Pereira, visitors will find history carefully preserved amongst ceramic remains, intricate arches and detailed mosaics. With the esteemed Carmo Archaeological Museum on site, many startling medieval artefacts await to be discovered, including the tomb of King Ferdinand I and two South American mummies.

🕐 M–Sa: 1000–1900 (Jun–Sep), –1800 (Oct–May)
💲 €4/3 🏠 Lgo. do Carmo, 1200–092
📞 +351 21 347 8629
🔗 www.museuarqueologicodocarmo.pt

"The imposing nave without a roof is an authentic union of interior and exterior space. The symbolic meaning of the space is magical."
– Miguel Marcelino

10 Igreja de São Vicente de Fora
Map C, P.107

Originally planned for a site outside the now-crumpled city walls, the "Church of St. Vincent Outside the Walls" is a prime example of Mannerist architecture and the resting ground of many Portuguese monarchs. Italian architect Filippo Terzi revised this impressive construction in 1627, visualising the identical bell towers and a symmetrical façade. Restored in 1855 after bearing the brunt of the infamous earthquake, visitors will find expansive historical azulejo panels depicting war scenes and fables across the monastery's rooms and passageways. Admire the varying types of marble that decorate the sacristy, and witness the beauty of the main altarpiece surrounded by many statues.

🕐 0900–2000 (M-Sa),
–1230, 1500–1700 (Su)
🏠 Lgo. São Vicente, 1100–572
📞 +351 21 882 4400

"Don't miss the medieval cistern, the terrace and the views."

– Ricardo Bak Gordon

11 **Museu do Teatro Romano**
Map D, P.107

Opened to the public in 2015, the Roman Theatre Museum houses the breathtaking remains
of one of the city's oldest theatres built during
the height of the Roman Empire. Dating back
to the first century, the theatre was thought to
have a 5,000-spectator capacity and rediscov-
ered in 1798, 44 years after the earthquake that
shattered the city. The only possible Roman
amphitheatre left in Portugal was not properly
excavated until the 1960s. Amongst impressive
stone columns and detailed sculptures, visitors
can discover an inscription dedicating the
theatre to Roman Emperor Nero, as well as a
statue of Greek mythological satyr Silenus.

🕐 1000–1800 (Tu–Su except Jan 1, May 1 & Dec 25)
💲 €3/1.50/free admission (Sundays before 1300,
May 18 & Jun 13) 🏠 R. de São Mamede 3A, 1100–532
📞 +351 21 817 2450 ⓊⓇⓁ www.museudelisboa.pt

"Enjoy a beautiful view of the city."
– Filipe Faísca

12 Fundação Calouste Gulbenkian

Map G, P.109

Enjoy both nature and art at The Calouste Gulbenkian Foundation and Museum in central Lisbon where large concrete structures mesh with lush greenery. The vision of architects Ruy Jervis d'Athouguia, Pedro Cid and Alberto Pessoa, this architectural wonder pays homage to the late businessman and philanthropist Calouste Gulbenkian, with an art library, auditoriums and a modern art museum to showcase his epic art collection. Try your luck attending a concert at the Grand Auditorium which puts on a scenic backdrop at times. Jazz fans visiting in August should check out their 10-day special programme Agosto that features open-air concerts, conferences and films.

🕐 0900-1300, 1430-1730 (M-F)
🏠 Av. de Berna 45A, 1067-001 📞 +351 21 782 3000
🔗 gulbenkian.pt 🎟 Museum: 1000-1800 (W-M), €10/free (Sundays from 2pm)

"Go on a sunny day so that you can get some sun in the garden. Eat on site or go to Oasis Vegetariano across the road for some decent vegetarian food."

– Hélio Morais, HAUS

Cultural & Art Spaces

Multipurpose spaces, independent galleries and thriving street art

The legacies of Portugal's signature art forms are ever present in Lisbon, and provide an important backdrop to the many new galleries and initiatives taking over unused spaces. The melancholic sounds of fado – the sentimental folk music native to Portugal – and bejewelled apartments baring age-old azulejos can be uncovered simply through walking down the city's winding cobbled streets.

Renowned institutions like the otherworldly Espaço Espelho d'Água (#18) or the fine art haven Museu Coleção Berardo (#13) facilitate a more formal encounter with Lisbon's art offerings, but other budding art spots certainly pack as much punch. Explore the colourful explosion of contemporary urban-inspired art inside Underdogs Gallery (#21), which also coordinates fascinating tours of the city's street art culture, whereas Galeria Pedro Alfacinha (#22) turns over multiple exhibitions per year with the best international talent, Galeria Vera Cortês (#20) offers great art books alongside its gallery, and Rua das Gaivotas 6 (#19) pulls together thought-provoking film, theatre, dance and seminars. Lisbon's street art has too garnered an ever-growing following of its own, with Barrio Alto and Picaos Metro Station's neighbouring areas constantly bursting with astounding murals.

Sara Westermann
Graphic designer

I'm a multidisciplinary designer specialising in poster, editorial design, illustration, and hand-lettering. I love working with different mediums. Unexpected results keep me motivated.

Teatro Nacional D.Maria II P.037

José Mata
Actor

I'm an actor and have been in theatre, television and cinema for over a decade. I love Lisbon. The weather, food, landscapes, and people make Lisbon perfect for both living and visiting.

Bruno Cardoso aka Xinobi
Co-founder, Discotexas

I'm Bruno Cardoso. I make music under the name Xinobi, play regularly all over the world, and run music label, Discotexas. I'm a nice grown-up kid who loves food.

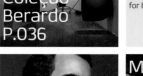

Museu Coleção Berardo P.036

Galeria Zé dos Bois P.038

Francisco Fino
Gallerist

I collaborate with galleries and museums to build a close relationship with artists, cura-tors, and theorists engaged with the internationalisation of contemporary art.

Museu Nacional de Etnologia P.041

Rita João & Pedro Ferreira
Co-founders, Pedrita

Pedrita is a multidisciplinary design studio founded in 2005. Their projects cast an inquisi-tive look on logic, the material culture, as well as questioning processes.

Gonçalo Campos
Product designer

Gonçalo Campos prides himself on finding surprising solutions through sound combination of materials and production methods, and a signature mix of humour and pragmatism

Appleton Square P.040

Espaço Espelho d'Água P.042

Joana Barrios
Actress & producer

I am Joana Barrios and I try to
live as many lives as possible.
Currently, I am a mother, wife,
actress, writer, and art director.

Galeria Vera Cortês P.045

Pauline Foessel
Co-director, Underdogs Gallery

Originally from France, Pauline
Foessel manages Vhils' studio
and an ambitious artistic programme which has put Lisbon
on the map of urban-inspired
contemporary art.

Kalaf Epalanga
Co-founder, Enchufada

I am an Angolan writer and
musician. I co-founded record
label Enchufada, a creative and
dynamic platform promoting
Global Club Music around the
world.

Rua das Gaivotas 6 P.044

Underdogs Gallery P.046

Carolina Pimenta
Visual artist

After working in New York on
an array of projects involving
production, video and photography, I started travelling in
hopes to capture a different
side of the world.

Miguel Jus-
tino Contem-
porary Art
P.048

HIBU.
Fashion label

We are Marta Gonçalves and
Gonçalo Páscoa, the duo behind
the unisex fashion design HIBU.,
founded in 2012. Since then,
we have been trying to break
boundaries in the fashion world.

Francisca Ramalho
Illustrator

Being an illustrator is a big part
of what I am. Thinking and
dreaming through shapes,
colours and realities lead me to
travel to worlds created by us
without being ours.

Galeria Pedro Alfacinha P.047

Carpe Diem Arte e Pesquisa P.049

13 Museu Coleção Berardo
Map E, P.108

Portuguese businessman, stock investor and art aficionado Joe Berardo is the man behind this astonishing collection of 20th- and 21st-century fine art, with modern masterpieces spanning Surrealism, Pop Art, Minimalism and conceptualism. Since 2007, over 1,000 world-renowned pieces jointly valued at 316 million euro have been showcased and preserved at the exhibition space in Lisbon's Cultural Centre of Belém. View legendary works by Marcel Duchamp, Andy Warhol and Pablo Picasso alongside temporary exhibitions featuring up-and-coming contemporary artists.

🕓 1000–1900 daily except Dec 25, –1430 (Dec 24 & 31), 1200–1900 (Jan 1)
🏠 Pc. do Império, 1449–003
☎ +351 21 361 2878
🔗 www.museuberardo.pt

"Don't miss the famous Portuguese dessert at Pastéis de Belém nearby!"

– Sara Westermann

14 Teatro Nacional D. Maria II
Map A, P.105

It would be hard to tell the ill-fated history that haunts D. Maria II National Theatre from its grandiose exterior. Occupying centre stage at Rossio Square, Portugal's national theatre is a stunning 19th-century Neoclassical building, although a week after a performance of Shakespeare's *Macbeth* in 1964 saw the whole building fall victim to flames, save the outer walls. Reopened some 14 years later with care taken to restore the interior's original designs, the theatre has since hosted many plays, exhibitions and other cultural happenings.

🕐 Show time vary with programme 💲 €5-17
🏠 Pc. dom Pedro IV, 1100-201
📞 +351 21 325 0800
URL www.tndm.pt
🔖 Guided tour: €8/4, Prior booking up to 5 days

"The building itself is a must-see. Watch a show here. Lisbon has plenty of directors and actors who are some of the best in Europe. You won't regret it."

– José Mata

⏱ Ⓢ *Opening hours & admission vary with events*
🏠 *R. da Barroca 59, 1200-049*
📞 *+351 21 343 0205*
🔗 *www.zedosbois.org*

15 Galeria Zé dos Bois

Map A, P.104

Sonic Youth's Thurston Moore, artist Emory Douglas and intellectual Jean Baudrillard are amongst a slew of cultural icons that have graced the arts programme at Galeria Zé dos Bois. Spanning 2,500 square metres, the non-profit is housed within an 18th-century palace, facilitating genre-bending exhibitions, performances, live music, film, and lectures since its opening in 1994. Famed for its celebration of international artists as well as homegrown talents, the centre hosts over 150 events every year, guaranteeing a memorable visit whatever the season, day and night.

"Here is a good plan: head for exhibitions, go to dinner and come back for one of their thought-provoking music shows."

– Bruno Cardoso aka Xinobi, Discotexas

16 Appleton Square
Map F, P.108

More than just a gallery, theatre or cultural centre, Appleton Square is all three combined and more – an innovative art space where creativity in all forms is nurtured and exhibited. This multipurpose vicinity stages experimental art performances and holds exhibitions across photography, installation and sculpture. Visitors will also find insightful architecture and art courses throughout the year, covering topics ranging from concrete structures to the history of Lisbon parishes. Check for what's happening on their Facebook page.

🕐 1400–1900 (Tu–Sa)
🏠 R. Acácio de Paiva 27, 1700-004
📞 +351 21 099 3660
📘 Appleton Square
🔗 www.appletonsquare.pt

"One of the most interesting aspects of this project is its very good yet versatile programme."
– Francisco Fino

17 Museu Nacional de Etnologia
Map K, P.110

Over 40,000 age-old artefacts and photographs chart Portugal's archaeological and ethnographic history at the National Museum of Ethnology in the scenic district of Belém. Founded in 1965, this vast concrete repository displays rare objects from Portugal's rural and colonial past, with its permanent exhibition *The Museum, Many Things* showcasing astonishing items spanning Portuguese folk instruments, Malian masks and Angolan dolls. Research enthusiasts will find the multimedia library a gold mine of extraordinary books, videos and classical recordings, whilst the drawing sessions, tapestry workshops and native-history courses will serve visitors' interests of a hands-on experience.

🕐 1400-1800 (Tu), 1000- (W–Su) $ €3
🏠 Av. Ilha da Madeira, 1400-203
📞 +351 21 304 1160, +351 21 304 1169
URL mnetnologia.wordpress.com
🖊 Guided tours: 1030, 1230, 1430, 1630 (W–Su), advance booking required

"If you want a quiet tour, this is where you can go and learn about the Portuguese culture through an impressive collection of objects and traditions."

– Gonçalo Campos

18 Espaço Espelho d'Água
Map E, P.108

Restored to its original 1940 characteristics in 2014, this hyper-modernist white structure extending out into the Tagus River could be mistaken for a sci-fi movie set piece. Named Espaço Espelho d'Água which translates as "Water Space Mirror", this restaurant and cultural haven unites the contemporary with the otherworldly, offering forward-thinking art, design and gastronomical experiences. Encounter expertly cooked cuisine from as far as Mozambique and Timor whilst marvelling at its kitchen covered by over 50 tropical plant species. The centre's weekly jazz night presents the genre's foremost performers.

🕐 1100-0000 (Su-Th), -0100 (F-Sa)
🏠 Av. Brasília 210, 1400-038 📞 +351 21 301 0510
URL espacoespelhodeagua.com

"Try Romeu e Julieta or Bolo de Rolo for dessert."
– Rita João & Pedro Ferreira, Pedrita

19 Rua das Gaivotas 6
Map B, P.106

A cultural centre dedicated to theatre, dance, cinema, exhibitions and debates, Rua das Gaivotas 6 is a creative sanctuary art-directed by artist collective Teatro Praga with a single aim – to accommodate the experimentations of young artists who wish to develop and showcase their projects. As such, no visit to this former school building is the same. With pastel walls and modern furnishings, this stunning space has staged a plethora of successful plays and performances since 2013, from theatrical adaptations to student shows. Scan through the online calendar prior to your visit to plan an evening of surprising encounters.

🕐 🅂 *Opening hours & admission vary with programmes*
🏠 *R. das Gaivotas 6, 1200-202*
📞 *+351 21 096 2355*
URL *ruadasgaivotas6.pt*

"Its doors are wide open to whoever wants to come on over to see the shows and integrate into the community."

– Joana Barrios

20 Galeria Vera Cortês
Map F, P.108

The most exciting emerging artists from Portugal and abroad grace the walls of Vera Cortês Gallery throughout the year, with its incredible roaster the envy of the gallery circuit. Championing tastemakers in painting, photography and fine art since 2003, the forward-thinking platform showcases regular solo and group shows, featuring work from visual artists such as Detanico Lain, João Queiroz and Vhils (P.070). The specially curated bookshop is a particular highlight, with limited editions, art monographs and international magazines on offer.

🕐 1400–1900 (Tu–F), 1000–1300, 1400–1900 (Sa) & by appointment except P.H. & August
🏠 R. João Saraiva 16, 1º, 1700-250
📞 +351 21 395 0177
URL www.veracortes.com

"Vera is a very good curator and her gallery hosts some of the best shows I've ever seen. I really like her taste."
– Pauline Foessel, Underdogs Gallery

21 Underdogs Gallery
Map I, P.110

Pioneering "urban-inspired graphic and visual culture" since 2010, Underdogs is a cultural platform at the forefront of Lisbon's underground art scene. Taking the guise of a gallery, art shop and tour programme, this comprehensive project exposes the city's ever-expanding urban art landscape from multiple perspectives. Discover emerging international talent or browse the art store for original artworks before grabbing a caffeine fix at the ground floor coffee shop. Keen to see how Lisbon artists are decorating the streets? Attend an Underdogs public art tour to discover the incredible large-scale murals that colour the capital.

🕐 1400–2000 (Tu–Sa)
📍 R. Fernando Palha, Armazém 56, 1950–132
📞 +351 21 868 0462
URL www.under-dogs.net

"The Underdogs Public Art Programme transformed Lisbon's streetscape by facilitating work by Vhils, How & Nosm, PixelPancho and many more."
– Kalaf Epalanga, Enchufada

22 Galeria Pedro Alfacinha
Map A, P.105

The brainchild of young Lisbon-native Pedro Alfacinha, this young gallery nestled on the historic Rua de São Mamede focuses on forward-thinking photographers, both established and emerging. Floored with terracotta tiles and gated by a mammoth black arched door, Galeria Pedro Alfacinha continuously provides a charming stage for its short and frequent exhibitions. Whether it's the stunning landscape shots of Los Angeles-based John Divola or António Júlio Duarte's gritty everyday observations, visitors are sure to be amazed.

🕐 1500–2100 (W–Sa)
📍 R. de São Mamede 25C, 1100–533
📞 +351 21 135 9220
🔗 pedroalfacinha.pt

"This young gallery is full of charm. Walk around that area after your visit and also go across the street to Caulino (#31)."

– Carolina Pimenta

23 Miguel Justino Contemporary Art
Map A, P.104

Formally known as Bloco103, this contemporary art gallery occupies a stunning ten-room location at Rua Rodrigues Sampaio, a stone's throw from the dazzling parade of designer stores in Avenida da Liberdade. Gallery director and proprietor Miguel Justino fills the space with the works of emerging and established Portuguese artists, such as the intricate drawings by Ana Velez and colourful paintings by Pedro Batista. Forward-thinking and innovative, art-lovers will come to appreciate Lisbon's exciting creative scene and the homegrown artists leading the way.

🕐 1300–1900 (Tu–F), 1500– (Sa, by appointment only)
🏠 R. Rodrigues Sampaio 31, 1º Esq., 1150–292
📞 +351 96 408 1283
URL www.galeriamigueljustino.com

"If you love contemporary art, this is the place to go!"
– Gonçalo Páscoa & Marta Gonçalves, HIBU.

24 Carpe Diem Arte e Pesquisa
Map A, P.104

The majestic setting of this 17th century palace lends itself well to the international and national contemporary art exhibited across its floors. Renovated after the 1755 earthquake, the not-for-profit centre has provided a site for academic research, visual arts and creative experimentation since 2009, attracting students, teachers, artists and art fanatics from across the world. Conferences, talks, tours and masterclasses offer a prime incentive tap into Lisbon's buzzing art scene.

🕐 1300–1900 (W–Sa except P.H.)
📍 R. de O Século 79, 1200–433
📞 +351 21 197 7102
URL www.carpe.pt

"This place is a love relationship between the past and the present."
– Francisca Ramalho

Markets & Shops

Legendary markets, charming boutiques and artisanal goods

A true marker of Portugal's charm is the retro packaging of its heritage brands. Whether it's sardine tins, soaps, toothpastes or oils, the most mundane products transform into covetable souvenirs. It's this attention to detail and respect for the past that characterises Lisbon's diverse offerings, where a long history of craftsmanship and artisanal traditions are embraced by established storefronts and an array of exceptional markets. Pay a visit to Loja da Burel (#27) for clothes and accessories made out of wool native to the country's mountainous regions, and marvel at the extensive collection of Portuguese brands at A Vida Portuguesa (#34) for treasured goods like Brito soaps and Benamôr Cream. Find ceramic perfection at Cortiço & Netos (#25), which sells the most astounding selection of intricately designed tiles in the city. A rewarding time can be had practising your haggling skills at the many markets too – Alfama's Feira da Ladra (*Campo de Santa Clara, 1100–472*) is a top spot that has been running since the 12th century, selling antiques, ceramics and furniture every Tuesday and Saturday. Ribeira Market (#41) is a key destination for stunning flowers, seasonal veg, fruit and fresh bread, whilst Biological Market (#35) celebrates natural organic products and produce. Fashion and interiors junkies won't be disappointed to find a range of independent shops and famed luxury outlets – Alexandra Moura (#29), Fabrica (#30) and Caulino (#31) are great spots.

Inês Revés
Journalist

I'm a design journalist who has contributed to *Frame*, *Domus*, *Disegno*, *Metropolis* and *Damn*. I studied product design and did a Master's in Design Cultures in Amsterdam for two years.

Cortiço & Netos
P.054

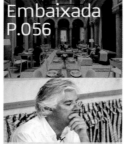

Embaixada
P.056

João Santa-Rita
Partner, Santa-Rita Arquitectos

Besides leading projects across the world, João Santa-Rita also teaches at Universidade Autónoma de Lisboa and is the president of the Portuguese Architectural Association.

P-06 atelier
Multidisciplinary design studio

Founded in 2006, P-06 atelier has conceived projects from complex, large-scale wayfinding systems and exhibition design, to communication and editorial design for the printed page.

Loja da Burel
P.057

Joana Vasconcelos
Artist

Born in Paris in 1971, Joana Vasconcelos has exhibited regularly since the mid-1990s. After her participation in The Venice Biennale in 2005, her work became known internationally.

Filipe Faísca
P.058

Alexandra Moura
P.059

Alexandra Moura
Fashion designer

I love creating new universes and showing them through my work. I am a lover of Lisbon, my city, and its bright lights.

Elsa Rodrigues
Graphic designer

I am a multidisciplinary designer with a soft spot for editorial design. My work bounces between different graphic disciplines such as illustration, art direction, graphic and web design.

Fabrica Features Lisboa
P.060

José Avillez
Chef & restaurateur

I am passionate about my country. I own seven restaurants, including Michelin-starred Belcanto and latest addition, BECO. When I'm not cooking, I host my own TV cooking show.

Louie Louie
P.062

Luis Clara Gomes
Musician, producer & DJ

With my project Moullinex I am fortunate to be able to travel the globe all year round, and bring my music to all sorts of audiences and settings.

Joana Areal
Co-founder, Thisislove Studio

Joana Areal works to deepen mankind's ability to communicate through diverse media and apprehend new languages within the practice of design.

Caulino
Ceramics
P.061

STET Livros &
Fotografias
P.063

Mercado
Biológico do
Príncipe Real
P.065

Teresa Freitas
Photographer

I like seeing the moon during the day, movies based on true stories and lemonade. I'm an avid Instagrammer who enjoys capturing the mystery of an unknown reality.

Ricardo Carvalho
Architect

Ricardo Carvalho is one half of architecture firm Ricardo Carvalho + Joana Vilhena. Their built projects include public buildings and the Museum of Design and Fashion in Lisbon.

José Adrião
Founder, José Adrião Arquitetos

Along with several buildings completed in housing, public, urban and ephemeral, José Adrião also teaches at Universidade Autónoma de Lisboa and co-directed Jornal Arquitectos.

A Vida
Portuguesa
P.064

LX Factory
P.066

25 Cortiço & Netos
Map A, P.105

Hundreds of tiles bearing intricate patterns and colour schemes are on display at Cortiço & Netos, nestled in Mouraria district. Pedro, João, Ricardo and Tiago Cortiço – the brothers who run the shop champion their grandfather's lifelong commitment to collect discontinued Portuguese industrial tiles. These delicate pieces of history, dating back to the 1960s, are showcased on pine shelving, amongst a diverse selection of ceramic homeware. Part of the Association for the Interpretation of the Industrial Tile, the shop reinvests all profits in the business and the upholding of its collection.

🕐 1000–1300, 1400–1900 (M–Sa)
🏠 Cc. de Santo André 66, 1100–497
📞 +351 21 136 2376   f Cortiço & Netos
URL corticoenetos.com

"*These are the best souvenir to take from Lisbon! They have it all: authenticity, tradition and history.*"

– Inês Revés

FIGURATIVO FIGURATIVE

26 Embaixada
Map A, P.104

An influx of creative start-ups and independent businesses have elevated Príncipe Real into Lisbon's "cool capital", with Embaixada concept store spearheading the area's cultural makeover since its opening in 2013. Mini retail spaces are spread over two floors within this former palace, where visitors can shop amongst Portugal's most exciting fashion, music, art, food and lifestyle brands, such as DOT and Organii Bebé. Wander across the first floor's exhibitions and events space after a session of retail therapy, and satisfy appetites at Atalho Real, open till midnight.

🏠 Pc. d. Príncipe Real 26, 1250
📞 +351 96 530 9154
URL www.embaixadalx.pt

"*It's a unique appropriation of a Moorish-style private palace from the 19th century, with a marvellous patio inside and view of the hills.*"

– João Santa-Rita, Santa-Rita Arquitectos

27 Loja da Burel
Map D, P.107

Devoted to reviving an otherwise dying trade since production went underway in 2010, Loja da Burel in picturesque Chiado is a quaint shop with big ambitions. All of their products are made out of wool fabrics prepared in their factory set amongst the Serra da Estrela mountain ranges, which is also worth a visit. Burel's standouts include its namesake, a strong and versatile traditional material handmade with pure wool. With new garments and objects by homegrown designers released throughout the year, this is the perfect spot for purchasing an authentic Portuguese gift.

🕐 1000–2000 (M–Sa), 1100–1900 (Su)
🏠 R. Serpa Pinto 15B, 1200–443
📞 +351 21 245 6910
f @BurelFactory

"Explore Chiado!"
– P-06 atelier

28 Filipe Faísca
Map B, P.106

Filipe Faísca's distinctive eye has seen him create clothing for theatre actors, opera performers, restaurant staff and a style-savvy public (P.013). One of the country's foremost fashion designers, the Mozambique-born powerhouse has earned undisputed renown since launching his first collection in 1991. With a string of awards to his name, including the Portuguese Golden Globes, a visit to his shop in Bairro Alto is a must. Stop by to collect some of the season's most forward-thinking contemporary designs.

🕙 1000-1300, 1400-1900 (M-F),
1230-2000 (Sa, by appointment only)
🏠 Cc. do Combro 99, 1200-112
📞 +351 21 342 0014
🔗 www.filipefaisca.com

"He is just great at knowing how to dress a woman."
– Joana Vasconcelos

29 Alexandra Moura
Map A, P.104

Luxurious fabrics and asymmetrical silhouettes characterise Moura's experimental collections. Daring yet surprisingly easy to wear, these versatile garments make a modern addition to a contemporary wardrobe. Find chic dresses, structured shirts and statement accessories displayed against an all-white interior in Príncipe Real, the home of her store and atelier since 2012. Take some time to discover the antique shops and galleries snuggled amongst the beautiful town houses nearby. The little garden across the road provides a calming retreat from the busy district.

🕙 1000–1900 (M–F)
🏠 Embaixada, Pc. do Príncipe Real 26, 2°, 1250–184
☎ +351 21 099 0712
🌐 www.alexandramoura.com

"This is where I create. Beyond my collections, appreciate its interior architecture while exploring the many products made by artists from across Portugal."

– Alexandra Moura

30 **Fabrica Features Lisboa**
Map D, P.107

Journey four flights up the Benetton megastore on Rue Garrett to find Fabrica, the creative product design offshoot from Benetton Group. Featuring an expertly curated selection of stationery, ceramics, tableware, glassware and accessories crafted by domestic and international artists, this retail space is part of a global network of three outlets celebrating innovation and craftsmanship. Since its inception in 2001, Fabrica has coupled its commercial offerings with an exhibition space too, dedicated to experimental product design, performances and launches. Keep an eye on their Facebook page to see what events are on the horizon.

🕐 1000–2000 (M–Sa), 1100–1900 (Su)
🏠 R. Garrett 83, Edifício Megastore Benetton, 4° Andar, 1200–203
📞 +351 21 342 0596
📘 @fabricalisboa
🔗 www.fabricafeatures.com

"Inside the store you will find small exhibitions and art/design–driven publications available for reading."
– Elsa Rodrigues

31 Caulino Ceramics

Map A, P.105

Caulino's founder Catia Pessoa has a long-term fascination for handcrafted ceramics that fuse traditional and contemporary design. Having studied the art for many years, Pessoa opened the shop and studio in 2006 in central Lisbon, gathering beautifully designed ornaments by young artists and established artisans across the country. Marvel at the tropical-coloured vases and huge ceramic balloons at the store, or try your hand at making a unique piece at their popular weekly classes.

🕐 1100–1800 (M–F)
🏠 R. de S. Mamede ao Caldas 28A, 1100–535
📞 +351 91 244 7703
f @caulinoceramics

"Book a one-day workshop in advance if you have the time!"

– José Avillez, Belcanto & BECO

32 Louie Louie
Map D, P.107

Led by pioneering record dealer Jorge Dias since 2013, Louie Louie is a haven for music fanatics after a rare gem. A large basement enclave in downtown Lisbon stocking second-hand CDs and vinyl, the shop prides itself on its extensive selection of rock, jazz, dance, Brazilian and fado – a quintessential Portuguese genre with roots in soul and folk. With knowledgeable staff on hand at all times, pass by the capital's most treasured record store for a leisurely browse and visit the small in house coffee shop for a homely brew.

🕐 1100–1930 (M–Sa), 1500– (Su & P.H.)
🏠 Escnh. do Santo Espírito da
Pedreira 3, 1100–225
📞 +351 21 347 2232
URL www.louielouie.biz

"Do spend time digging and bring something home, like the Brazilian and African music that brims over the used crates."
– Luis Clara Gomes, Moullinex

33 STET Livros & Fotografias
Map B, P.106

STET sits on the first floor of a stunning 18th-century build in the heart of Chiado. A central hub championing innovative photography publishing, this specialised bookstore has acquired a phenomenal selection of photo books, artist books, independent publications, rare editions and prints since its opening in 2011, with releases from MACK, Steidl, AKINA and kameraphoto amongst its extensive inventory. The store also stages events and launches for domestic and international publishers, whilst also heading up EDIT – a new summer book fair showcasing the work of 30 handpicked publishers and authors.

🕐 *1530–1930 (Th–F) or by appointment*
🏠 *R. do Norte 14, 1º Andar, 1200–286*
📞 *+351 91 752 0046*
URL *stet-livros-fotografias.com*

"For photography, design, independent publishing and author books lovers, STET is the place to visit."

– Joana Areal, Thisislove Studio

34 A Vida Portuguesa
Map A, P.105

Offering heritage Portuguese brands in a contemporary setting, A Vida Portuguesa is a treasure trove charting the nation's independent manufacturing history. Born out of a desire to celebrate, preserve and reintroduce Portugal's forgotten products, journalist Catarina Portas opened the shop in 2004 with a catalogue of items that have enchanted visitors throughout the years. After a truly unique souvenir? Peruse the Ach. Brito soaps, Algarve sea salt, Benamôr cream, Serrote notepads and the many adorable books, jewellery and kitchenware on offer. Make sure you have plenty of time to look around.

🕐 1030–1930 daily
🏠 Flagship: Lgo. do Intendente Pina Manique 23, 1100–285
📞 +351 21 197 4512
🌐 www.avidaportuguesa.com

"Take home with you a ceramic piece of the Portuguese artist Rafael Bordalo Pinheiro. You won't find anything like it, anywhere else."
– Teresa Freitas

35 Mercado Biológico do Príncipe Real

Map A, P.104

Passionate farmers from across the country come to Príncipe Real to sell their fresh organic produce to an enthusiastic public. Homemade olive oil, artisan breads and jams are sold alongside a variety of seasonal fruits and vegetables, all of which infuses this market with vivid hues and mouth-watering smells. Open every Saturday in Príncipe Real Park, foodies will find high quality produce in abundance, most of which can be sampled before purchase. Prices can be quite steep so don't be afraid to bargain for a better deal. For a smooth-sailing morning of shopping, arrive early to avoid the crowds and end your trip with a light brunch at one of the open-air cafés that line the park.

🕐 *0900–1500 (Sa)*
🏠 *Pc. do Príncipe Real, 1250–096*

"Unlike other European cities where open-air markets are more common, it is quite unique in Lisbon."
– Ricardo Carvalho, Ricardo Carvalho + Joana Vilhena

36 LX Factory
Map H, P.109

Cited as Lisbon's "creative island", LX Factory is a 23,000-square-metre former fabric factory crammed with independent retailers and swarming with young artists. Unsure where to start in this mammoth arty playground? Head to one of Portugal's most stunning bookstores, Ler Devagar, where publications are piled from floor to ceiling. Or grab a creamy slice of Madame Cheeselova's homemade cheesecakes at LXeeseCake. To view this industrial compound in its full glory, attend the annual Open Day in the month of May or November, where over 150 resident artists showcase their stunning projects, alongside yoga and dance workshops, talks and performances.

🏠 R. Rodrigues de Faria 103, 1300-501
☎ +351 21 314 3399
URL www.lxfactory.com

"It's worth roaming through the ancient corridors of the converted factory. Ler Devagar on the main street is one of the most charismatic bookstores in Lisbon."
– José Adrião Arquitectos

Restaurants & Cafés

Hearty classics, prime seafood and fusion cuisine

Lisboners will attest to the international influences that are permeating the city's delicious cuisine, though the heart of Portuguese cooking remains firmly at the core. In fact, the city's culinary culture pioneers with its talent for fusion without compromise. Tasca Kome (#39) transforms home-reared ingredients with Japanese preparations – the soy gravy pork belly and aubergine fries firm favourites. Naturally, seafood dishes are the forte of the coastal capital; order *bacalhau* (salted cod fish), tender calamari and seasoned shellfish to get a true taste of the Atlantic. Café do Monte's (#45) generous sharing platters of freshly caught marine specialities are perfect for sharing amongst a small group – but don't forget to try the meat and cheese boards too. A more refined dining experience can be had at the Michelin star-winning Belcanto (#38), revered for its 21st century take on Portuguese classics whilst Sala de Corte (#37) will satisfy carnivores with grilled tenderloin and steaks accented with truffle oil. Of course, don't miss out on the simple classics – a decadent *bifana* (pork sandwich) can be devoured at Zé dos Cornos (#47) and Nata Tarts (custard tarts) are served in most cafés.

MusaWorkLab
Design consultancy

Founded by Paulo Lima, Raquel Viana and Ricardo Alexandre, MusaWorkLab creates with a network of creative professionals with diverse backgrounds and talent.

Belcanto
P.074

Henrique Sá Pessoa
Chef & restauranteur

I co-own Michelin-starred ALMA and Cais da Pedra. Besides my passion for food, I love travelling, music, being Portuguese and being privileged by our great weather, ocean, and beach.

Toyno Studio
Experience design studio

We are a brand that has fun creating products and spaces. Born in 2011 between Berlin and Lisbon, Toyno bears the hearts and imagination of six grown ups – sorry, six adults.

Sala de Corte
P.072

Tasca Kome
P.076

ADD FUEL
Illustrator & street artist

I am Diogo Machado. I create unique visual universes. Later in life, I redirected my attention to reinterpreting the language of traditional Portuguese azulejo design.

Time Out Market Lisboa
P.078

Alexandre Farto aka Vhils
Street artist

I grew up in Seixal, a suburban town across the river from Lisbon. Despite working in locations around the world, I still call Lisbon my home, where my main studio is.

Rui Vieira
Film director & photographer

For over ten years, I was a creative director at agencies like Fullsix, O Escritório and AKQA. Whilst there, I co-organised and produced OFFF Festival in Lisbon in 2008 and 2009.

Pizzeria-il Siciliano
P.077

Pinóquio
P.079

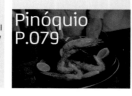

André Carrilho
Designer & Illustrator

I'm a cartoonist, animator, and caricaturist. I received several national and international prizes and have shown my work in Brazil, China, the Czech Republic, France, Portugal, Spain and USA.

Cantina das Freiras
P.081

Rui Pereira
Product designer

I explore the product typologies that immediately connect with users and raise awareness of contemporary issues. My travels reflect my interest in cultures. I currently live in Copenhagen.

Mariana Fernandes
Graphic designer & illustrator

Often process driven, I employ multiple disciplines and use varied skills to create. I split time between Fabrica Design Studio and my personal projects, in Treviso and Lisbon.

Gelateria Nannarella
P.080

Café do Monte
P.082

Studio AH–HA
Communication design studio

Catarina Carreiras and Carolina Cantante formed Studio AH–HA. The team adopts a holistic approach towards design and branding, and works with clients throughout the process.

Zé dos Cornos
P.084

vivóeusébio
Design collective

Founded in 2006, with offices in Lisbon and London, vivóeusébio focuses their creative energies on editorial and print design projects, from books and magazines, to posters and flyers.

Pedro Duarte Jorge
Photographer

Working with photography since 17, I love to build stories with images. I am a very curious person and photography offer me a way to observe the world.

Taberna da Rua das Flores
P.083

Zé da Mouraria
P.085

37 Sala De Corte
Map B, P.106

Ardent carnivores are welcome at Sala de Corte. Specialising in quality grills, this elegant restaurant seats 18 guests at the tables and ten diners at the marble bar – a prime location for curious eaters keen to observe the preparation of those splendid cuts. Since opening in 2015, Sala de Corte has amassed a legion of enthusiastic fans impressed by the distinctive flavour of their searing steaks sourced from local cattle breed producers. Ready for a meat feast? Try beef carpaccio with truffle oil or veal with Dijon mustard, two of the many dishes revered by its following.

🕐 1200–0000 daily
🏠 R. da Ribeira Nova 28, 1200-376
📞 +351 21 346 0030 🔗 www.saladecorte.pt
🖉 Closes between 3–7pm on weekdays.

"Try any of their pregos (Portuguese steak sandwich) made with bolo do caco, a flat bread from the Madeira Islands."

– MusaWorkLab

38 **Belcanto**
Map D, P.107

Belcanto's two Michelin stars are a testament to the elegance and refinement of this stylish establishment, founded in 1958. A history of artists' rendezvous and gentleman club antics predates Belcanto's current contemporary finesse, pioneered by young renowned chef José Avillez (P.053). Now, a sophisticated wood-panelled interior backdrops elaborate fa-vourites like Suckling Pig Revisited and Jackson Pollock Skate, available to wash down with an Inverted Martini or a bottle from a list of 300 wines. With only ten tables and countless five star reviews, a reservation is your ticket to the epitome of 21st century–haute cuisine.

🕐 1230–1500, 1900–2300 (Tu-Sa)
🏠 Lgo. de São Carlos 10, 1200–410
📞 +351 21 342 0607
URL belcanto.pt

 "*Their tasting menu is full of surprises. For a more casual experience, Peixaria da Esquina is a must for super fresh fish and great Portuguese recipes with a twist.*"

– Henrique Sá Pessoa, Alma, Cais da Pedra & Henrique Sá Pessoa

39 **Tasca Kome**
Map D, P.107

Japan expat and restaurant-owner Yuko
Yamamoto accents Portuguese dishes with
exotic flavours of her homeland. Since this
izakaya-style *tasca* (Portuguese tavern serving
inexpensive home-style food) opened in 2013,
diners have assigned high praise to its short
yet well-curated menu of *katsu* curry (deep-
fried pork), tender pork belly drenched in soy
gravy, flavourful sashimi, *onigiri* (rice balls) and
moreish aubergine fries on top of their friendly
service. Wash down your meal with *mugi-cha*
(barley tea) or delicious sake within this stylish,
dimly-lit interior in downtown Lisbon.

🕐 1200-1430, 1900-2200 (Tu-F),
1230-1500, 1900-2200 (Sa)
🏠 R. da Madalena 57, 1100-318
📞 +351 21 134 0117
URL www.kome-lisboa.com

"*Be sure to try the desserts, especially the Portuguese
influenced delicacy green tea castella sponge cake.*"
– Toyno Studio

40 Pizzeria-il Siciliano
Map P, P.111

Lisbon's answer to Italian cooking has found an unassuming outlet in this cosy restaurant on Rue do Poco Novo. The owner is Sicilian, so dubious diners set on authenticity will be pleasantly surprised by the light focaccias, creamy risottos, rich pasta dishes and thin-base pizzas topped with eggplant, parmigiano and olives. Open till late, the pizzeria's wine list features bottles from both Italy and Portugal, uniting the best of both worlds.

🕐 1200–1500, 1900–2300 (W–M)
🏠 R. do Poço Novo 138A, 2750-465
📞 +351 21 486 8357
URL ilsiciliano.pt

"This is one of, if not the best, Italian restaurant I've ever been to. My go-to place when I want comfort food."

– Diogo Machado aka ADD FUEL

41 Time Out Market Lisboa
Map B, P.106

Rescued from closure by the Time Out team in 2014, Mercado da Ribeira continues its legacy as a centre for great food and community. Serving native cuisine and fresh produce since the 13th century, this former market has evolved into Lisbon's top food court, decked with a staggering 40 some kiosks offering local specialties such as Azeitão cheese made from sheep's milk, *pregos* at O Prego da Peixaria, tartar prepared by Tartar-ia, Ginja wild cherry liqueur and Madeira wines. Santini ice-creams will be a nice finish to your meal.

🕐 1000–0000 (Su–W), –0200 (Th–Sa)
🏠 Av. 24 de Julho 49, Mercado da Ribeira, 1200–479
📞 +351 213 951 274
📘 @TimeOutMarketLisboa

"*Perfect for foodies. It also features a range of cool shops. Head there in the early morning if you want to catch the traditional market in full swing.*"
– Alexandre Farto aka Vhils

42 Pinóquio
Map A, P.105

Seafood lovers will find themselves abundantly satisfied with Pinóquio's famous Ria Formosa clams, crabs and lobster dishes. Sited in Restauradores Square, diners can expect a gastronomic experience that's picturesque, where stunning architecture and age-old sights set the tone. Meat-lovers will find the oven-baked duck rice and flame-broiled tenderloin steak particularly gratifying, whilst the appetiser menu – featuring prosciutto-wrapped melon and shrimp cocktails – is a surefire crowd pleaser. On a sunny day, make use of the restaurant's terrace to enjoy the weather and the square's busy ambiance.

🕐 1200–0000 daily
🏠 Pc. dos Restauradores 79, 1250-188
📞 +351 21 346 5106
URL restaurantepinoquio.pt

"You can't miss massada de marisco (seafood pasta) and pica-pau steak. Film fanatics can enjoy debates with their staff Antonio about any movie genres."

– Rui Vieira

43 **Gelateria Nannarella**
Map A, P.104

Gelateria Nannarella's five-star ratings and rave reviews are validated by their world-class gelato. Expect an indulgently dense dessert from this pastel-coloured ice-cream parlour, the vision of two Italian expats dedicated to authentic homemade recipes free of colouring and preservatives. There are up to 18 flavours available to cool off the summer heat, with tiramisu, pistachio, Oreo, mango and coffee on offer from the tiny storefront. Servings are incredibly generous here, with a medium cup or cone costing only three euros, so it's best advised to tackle the sweet treat on an empty stomach.

🕐 1200-2200 daily
🏠 R. Nova da Piedade 64, 1200-299
📞 +351 92 687 8553
📘 Gelateria Nannarella

"Try the basil or fig flavours! Their ice-cream is the best in town, all homemade."

– André Carrilho

44 Cantina das Freiras
Map D, P.107

Nicknamed "The Nun's Canteen", this semi-secret spot managed by a Catholic association pioneers a simple menu of Portuguese favourites that include rich gazpacho, sumptuous quiches and crispy fried cod. A mere seven euros will cover a main and dessert with change to spare, a lure for locals and curious tourists who enjoy tasty, generous plates that are easy on the pocket. On arrival, bypass the modest interior décor and dine on the roof terrace that looks out over the Tagus River and the city. The canteen ceases service at 3pm, so arrive early to secure a bargain lunch with a view.

🕐 *0830–1500 (M–F)*
🏠 *Tv. do Ferragial 1, 1200–182*
📞 *+351 21 324 0910*

"Whenever in town, I meet friends here for an easy lunch and a joyful sunbath. Just choose one of the homemade hot dishes and enjoy the view."

– Rui Pereira

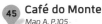

45 Café do Monte
Map A, P.105

Burgundy interiors are adorned with vintage film posters in this warm intimate café where diners can graze over *tábuas* (sharing platters of mostly fish, meat and cheese) whilst playing vintage board games. The goat cheese salad is recommended for a light meal, whilst the *crocantes* (crunchy toasts topped with serrano ham, cheese, or trout) are a perfect accompaniment with wine or a refreshing smoothie. A filling lunch or weekend brunch for two will cost around 25 euros, perfect for fuelling up before heading to Miradouro da Senhora do Monte (Our Lady of the Hill) – the city's highest lookout point for breathtaking panoramic views.

🕙 1100–0000 (Tu–Th), –0200 (F–Sa), –2330 (Su)
🏠 R. de São Gens 1, 1170–108
📞 +351 92 942 5156
📘 Café do Monte 🔗 Cash only

"The place is really relaxing so don't expect fast service. They have good homemade cakes and savouries. Ask for a delicious Croq Monsieur!"

– Mariana Fernandes

46 Taberna da Rua das Flores
Map B, P.106

Forget reservations and set menus – Taberna da Rua das Flores surprises every visit. New dishes are sprawled over the chalkboard daily, where *iscas* (marinated liver), duck rice, and various *petiscos* (Portuguese tapas) can be enjoyed within the small vintage style hole-in-the-wall. Locally-sourced ingredients form the basis of their simple yet full-flavoured offerings – a theme thoroughly embraced by passionate owner and founder André Magalhães. Go for late lunch or early dinner as bookings aren't taken here. When queues start to stretch, eager diners usually nurse a glass of wine to ease the waiting time.

🕐 1200-0000 (M-F), 1800- (Sa)
🏠 R. das Flores 103, 1200-194
f A Taberna da Rua das Flores

"Their food is almost a work of art, so we always go for big lunch breaks. Don't miss the chocolate cake and the house's signature broa (cornbread)."
– Studio AH–HA

47 Zé dos Cornos
Map A, P.105

Zé dos Cornos might not boast the glamour of the city's premier restaurants, but its family atmosphere and genuine home-cooked cuisine make it a perfect casual dining experience for those after a truly authentic fuss-free lunch. Hidden in a small alleyway between Rua da Madalena and Martim Moniz, this neighbourhood joint serves hearty chargrilled meat, salt cod and what many have named Lisbon's best *bifana* (a bun filled with thinly sliced richly-seasoned pork). With large portions a mainstay throughout the menu, diners might consider having just one to two dishes in one sitting.

🕐 1140–2200 (M–Sa)
🏠 Bc. dos Surradores 5, 1100–591
📞 +351 21 886 9641
📘 @ZeCornos

"Go on Tuesdays and go early because it will be packed with people going for ribs and rice with beans."

– vivóeusébio

48 Zé da Mouraria

Map A, P.105

Perched on the cobbled streets of this historic Moorish neighbourhood sits Zé da Mouraria, a classic Portuguese tavern known for its full-bodied comfort dishes. Generous portions of steak smothered in garlic and tender herbed Calamari are prepared lovingly in the open kitchen where a passionate team work to satisfy this ever-busy spot. It's not unusual for diners to take their leftovers home as a single portion can easily be shared amongst two. Bring cash, as credit cards aren't accepted here.

🕐 1200–1600 (M–Sa)
🏠 R. João do Outeiro 24, 1100–292
📞 +351 21 886 5436
🏷 Cash only

"Go around noon or 2.30pm to secure a table. It's my favourite restaurant in Lisbon. You feel like everyone working there loves their job."

– Pedro Duarte Jorge

Nightlife

Hidden clubs, wild raves and underground debauchery

It's not unusual to see the streets of Bairro Alto and Cais do Sodré buzzing with young creative types socialising with a drink in hand. Often cited as one of the most affordable and diverse nightlife destinations in Europe, Lisbon's ever-evolving club culture sees new bars and dance venues constantly popping up in place of neglected shops and empty warehouses. Swing by the acclaimed Musicbox Lisboa (#58) for soul, hip-hop, punk and reggae nights throughout the week and party with the city's most eclectic arty crowd in ZDB (#52) where the foosball area is perfect for some light-hearted fun. Like many capitals, expect a great selection of high-class spots, but don't let the exclusivity deter you – charm and a slick outfit can get you far. The grand dance floor at LuxFrágil (#59) is a regular haunt for A-listers so it's recommended you arrive early and in your best outfit. Pensão Amor's (#60) burlesque shows, pole-dancing performances and erotica bookstore is the perfect spot for debauchery and indulgent evenings. When drawing up your plans, factor a night for some jazz at the legendary Hot Club de Portugal (#54), famed as one of the best places to see the international pioneers of the distinctive music genre.

AKACORLEONE
Illustrator

AKACORLEONE's work is a frenzy of vivid colours, funny subject matters, and overprint effects. The contemporary style has made him a popular artist for shows, publications and events.

Casa Independente
P.092

Carminho
Singer

I'm Maria do Carmo. I sing fado since I was six following my mother. Lisbon is a beautiful city and I get inspired by the connections between different people from different places.

PARK
P.090

Maria Imaginário
Visual artist & illustrator

Known for painting colourful treats on decrepit buildings, Maria Imaginário develops a deeply personal visual universe using original languages with a bitter-sweet twist.

Mesa De Frades
P.093

Armando Ribeiro
Founder, O Apartamento

I'm the creative director of O Apartamento and a compulsive magazine buyer. I like travelling, photography, meet people and Asian food. Nature and free time are essential to my routine.

DAMAS
P.095

Pedro Duarte
Creative director, Havas

Pedro Duarte is a multidisciplinary Portuguese designer specialising in branding and illustration. Prior to Havas, he worked in Fluor Design, Bycom and BBDO/RMAC Brand Design.

v-a studio
Graphic & digital design studio

We create branding and graphic designs for both cultural and commercial clients, with offices in Lisbon and New York. We are also competitive table tennis players; come challenge us!

49 ZDB
P.094

Hot Club de Portugal
P.096

Joana Astolfi & João Pombeiro, *Studio Astolfi*

The duo focuses on architecture, interior design, art installations and custom-made pieces. Astolfi has a team of ten collaborators working in different projects.

TOPO
P.098

Carlos FOFI Cipriano
Filmmaker

I am also an "artistic handyman". I am more articulate with images than words, and I love to entertain. *Human Behaviour* by Michel Gondry inspired my artistic growth.

Paulo Condez
Founder, NADA design studio

I love Lisbon's light and its proximity to the sea. I also love its history and multiculturalism.

Sol e Pesca
P.097

Pavilhão
Chinês
P.099

The Legendary Tigerman
Musician

The Legendary Tigerman is all about the roots and the combining of new technologies, such as samples, beats and loops. However, playing instruments live is what brought him exposure.

LuxFrágil
P.101

RA\\STUDIO
Architectural duo

Luís and Tiago Rebelo de Andrade are a father and son duo from Lisbon. They work in both private and public sectors and have won several awards for their achievements.

Angela aka Kruella
Artist & Illustrator

A native Lisboner, I love to travel, make murals, exhibitions, and artistic residencies or any artistic intervention. I illustrated CITIx60 Lisbon's map jacket.

Musicbox
Lisboa
P.100

Pensão Amor
P.102

49 PARK

Map B, P.106

A grand 180-degree view and a peaceful garden terrace designed by Studio Astolfi (P.089) will generously reward a climb through Bairro Alto's seven-floor car park on Calçada do Combro. PARK's converted rooftop is an urban haunt for casual drinks, mean burgers and yearlong event roster featuring film screenings and outdoor raves. Open from 1pm till late, start your night with views of dusk settling over the city, accompanied with liberal jugs of Sangria. Tip - if you're not one to trek up multiple flights, take the lift to the fifth floor and walk up the relatively painless two levels.

🕐 1300–1500, 2000–2300 (Tu–F), –2300 (Sa), –2000 (Su)
🏠 Cc. do Combro 58, 1200-109
☎ +351 21 591 4011
f @parklisboaofficial

"The perfect place to hang out in the late afternoon, drink a mojito and be absorbed in one of the best views you can have in Lisbon's downtown area."

– AKACORLEONE

50 Casa Independente
Map A, P.105

Casa Independente revives the aura of the legendary grémios that were popular decades past – where drinks, conversation and partying combine to make the ultimate leisure haven. North of Martim Moniz, this former palace turned creative space is the brainchild of Ironia Tropical – a female collective whose concert planning found a permanent home here in 2012. Amongst energetic live shows, attendees can weave through the labyrinthine layout to fine the intimate lounge, café, bar and terrace – all thoughtfully decked with striking vintage furniture.

🕐 1400–0000 (M–F), 1200–0200 (Sa)
🏠 Lgo. do Intendente 45, 1100–285
📞 +351 21 887 2842
URL casaindependente.com

"It sits on a typical downtown square which is full of life. It has a lovely interior, making it a really nice place to have a drink, talk or dance."

– Maria Imaginário

51 Mesa De Frades
Map C, P.107

From chapel to food store to restaurant, Mesa De Frades' diverse history fosters a unique atmosphere, where fado music – popular Portuguese folk shanties – and rustic food combine within an 18th century blue-tiled interior that just went through a four-month refurb. For over a decade, musicians hit the stage at 11pm, and visitors come to either nibble over the fixed-price traditional menu or nurse a drink whilst watching the performances. Arrive at around 9pm to secure a table.

🕑 2000–0230 (M–Sa)
🏠 R. dos Remédios 139A, 1100–445
📞 +351 91 702 9436, mesadefrades@gmail.com
📘 @mesadefradeslisboa

"I started performing here when I was 17 until around 23 years old. In between tables you sing or you hear others sing."

– Carminho

 49 ZDB
Map A, P.104

Lisbon's quirky art crowd party hard at this fashionable nightspot joined to Galeria Zé dos Bois (#15). Concerts and DJ-led nights soundtrack wild evenings, where musicians, actors and artists amass together for dancing and raucous boozing. If the night gets too intense, revellers are welcome to play foosball, write on the walls or break for coffee before returning inside. Entry is reserved to members of ZDB or the neighbouring gallery, although new members are often admitted on the door.

 🕓 2200–0300 (F–Sa)
🏠 R. da Barroca 49, 1200–049
📞 +351 21 343 0205
f 49 ZDB

 "This place always has great gigs and very nice exhibitions. See the monthly agenda."
– Armando Ribeiro, O Apartamento

53 DAMAS
Map A, P.105

A café by day and a bar/music venue by night, DAMAS is a truly multipurpose hang out with something to offer at all hours. Formerly an industrial bakery, the 200–square–metre space is equal parts intimate and quirky, with its blue giraffe mural and fluorescent outdoor sign a testament to DAMAS' fun atmosphere. Delectable dishes like tuna ceviche and steak are amongst a range of vegan and vegetarian options, whilst a trip to the back hall for DJ sets and concerts will end the night on a high note.

🕐 1200–0200 (Tu), 1800– (W & Th), 1800–0400 (F), –0400 (Sa), 1700–0000 (Su)
🏠 R. da Voz do Operário 60, 1100–621
📞 +351 96 496 4416
f @DAMASLISBOA

"With great tapas and an eclectic line-up, from Afro music to jazz, this is an amazing place to go outside the bar area. Be ready for the unexpected!"
– v–a studio

54 Hot Club de Portugal
Map A, P.104

Portugal's famed jazz heritage starts here at
Hot Club de Portugal. Named one of the top
bars in the world to encounter the distinctive
genre, the cultural landmark has played host
to legendary jam sessions and mind-blowing
rhythmic performances since 1948 – making
it the country's oldest jazz club. Icons such as
Sarah Vaughan, Ronnie Scott and Max Roach
have all demonstrated their world-class talent
here, and though an unfortunate fire in 2009
shifted its location to a larger spot in the same
area of Praça da Alegria, its influence and
energy still remains in tact.

🕐 2200–0200 (Tu–Sa)
🏠 Pc. da Alegria 48, 1250–004
📞 +351 21 346 0305
URL www.hcp.pt

"*Enjoy the music and have a good time with friends.*"
– Pedro Duarte, Havas

55 Sol e Pesca
Map B, P.106

With walls lined with fishing rods, lines and hooks, Sol e Pesca's sea-themed décor harks back to its past life as a fisherman's hardware shop. Now, this quirky café/bar operates as a popular after dark hangout pulling in punters with an array of beers, wines and fish appetizers. Situated in the riverside clubbing district of Cais de Sodré, couple your beer with a delicious side of canned tuna, sardines or squid before descending onto the neighbouring night spots. Don't forget to purchase some tinned treats to go, they double as a great souvenir or gift.

🕐 1200–0200 (Su–Th), –0300 (F–Sa)
🏠 R. Nova do Carvalho 44, 1200-292
📞 +351 21 346 7203
f @solepesca

56 TOPO
Map A, P.105

An elevator ride six floors up a former retail warehouse will lead you to one of the city's best views spanning São Jorge Castle, Senhora do Monte and Martim Moniz Square. A sleek rooftop space showcasing Lisbon's skyline to stunning effect, TOPO is the perfect setting for after-hours socialising and romantic rendez-vous. With the interior and exterior designed by architects João Botelho and Miguel Oliveira,

visitors can graze on *Tártaro de novilho* (calf beef tartare), gyoza and *prego*, alongside an extensive drinks menu. Order the black pepper and basil cocktail for a summery treat and delight your taste buds with the lush dulce de leche mousse.

🕐 1230–0000 (Su–Th), –0200 (F–Sa)
🏠 R. Palma, Centro Comercial Martim Moniz, 6°, 1100–341
📞 +351 215 881 322
📘 TOPO

"*Enjoy the view over the city with an appetizer and good music.*"

– Paulo Condez, NADA design studio

57 Pavilhão Chinês
Map A, P.104

On entering the Pavilhão Chinês (Chinese Pavilion), visitors are welcomed into a weird and wonderful world adorned with all kinds of kitsch ephemera and treasures spanning miniature dolls, oil paintings and china tea sets. A cult bar masquerading as a quirky antique-filled museum, the venue is housed within a former grocery shop that specialised in far eastern spices, with its five rooms now covered in collectables and furnished with plush armchairs and sofas. Order fresh brew during the day and indulge in the extensive cocktail selection by night whilst admiring the many unique trinkets.

🕐 1800–0200 (M-Sa), 2100– (Su)
🏠 R. Dom Pedro V, 89/91, 1250–093
f @pavilhaochines

"A nice pit stop for a tea break or a cocktail. Smoking is allowed and the place has with two snooker tables, open till late."

– Carlos Cipriano aka FOFI

58 Musicbox Lisboa
Map B, P.106

Find Musicbox hidden beneath a large stone
arch in Cais do Sodré, a suitably atmospheric
location for one of Lisbon's most acclaimed
nightlife hotspots. Decked with a huge stage,
lounge and bar, the club has played host to an
array of live acts and themed nights across
varying genres since 2006. Serious music lovers
will be pleased to find soul, hip-hop, punk and
reggae events – all spun by Lisbon's finest –
splashed across Musicbox's packed schedule.
Most nights finish at 6am, and with a selection
of food outlets nearby, visitors are guaranteed a
lively evening.

🕐 💲 *Showtime & price vary with programmes*
🏠 R. Nova do Carvalho 24, 1200–292
📞 +351 21 343 0107
URL musicboxlisboa.com

*"Choose the night well. If possible, go for the night
when the infamous and legendary La Flama Blanca is
the Master of Ceremonies, e.g. Baile Tropicante."*
– Paulo Furtado aka The Legendary Tigerman

59 LuxFrágil
Map C, P.107

Extraordinary in both size and reputation, LuxFrágil is amongst Lisbon's largest night-clubs. A lavish dance floor, bar and terrace each occupy a single floor, with all levels bearing contemporary fittings and retro décor. Though varied in its musical offerings, electro music is the mainstay here, with famed DJs frequenting the decks. This fashionable haunt gets incredibly packed come 3am as A-listers and stylish professionals are steadily admitted, so arrive early and dress to impress to bypass the strict door policy.

🕐 2300–0600 (Th–Sa)
🏠 Av. Infante d. Henrique, Armazém A, Cais da Pedra a Sta Apolónia, 1950–376
📞 +351 21 882 0890
URL luxfragil.com

"Dancing until the morning to good music. What else do you need?"

– Angela aka Kruella

60 Pensão Amor
Map B, P.106

Pensão Amor is filled with trashy and flamboyant furniture from its brothel past, but that's part of the allure of this one-of-a-kind bar. Located in an 18th century five-storey address in the bustling area of Cais do Sodré, the "Love House" may seem like an unlikely contestant for popularity, but its specialist erotica bookstore, hair salon, concert space and pole dancing rooms make it an unmissable spot for locals and tourists winding through Rua Nova do Carvalho. Visit to get your fill of burlesque shows, live performances, alcoholic beverages and Peruvian-style cuisine.

🕐 1200–0300 (Su–W), –0400 (Th–Sa)
🏠 R. do Alecrim 19, 1200–014
📞 +351 21 314 3399
📘 @pensaoamor

"Rua Cor de Rosa (Pink Street), which is Rua Nova do Carvalho, is literally painted in pink. After Pensão Amor, hail a taxi and head to LuxFrágil (#59)."
– RA\\STUDIO

DISTRICT MAP : **SÃO BENTO, PRINCIPAL REAL, BAIRRO ALTO**

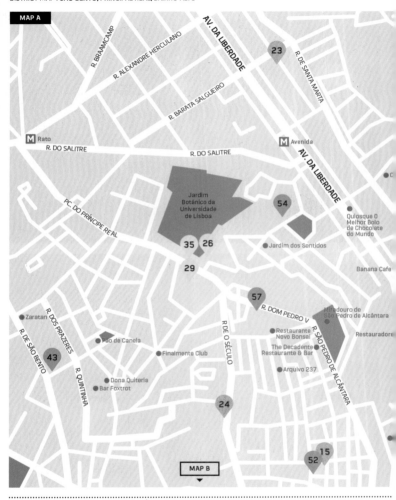

- 15_Galeria Zé dos Bois
- 23_Miguel Justino Contemporary Art
- 24_Carpe Diem Arte e Pesquisa
- 26_Embaixada
- 29_Alexandra Moura
- 35_Mercado Biológico do Príncipe Real
- 43_Gelateria Nannarella
- 52_49 ZDB
- 54_Hot Club de Portugal
- 57_Pavilhão Chinês

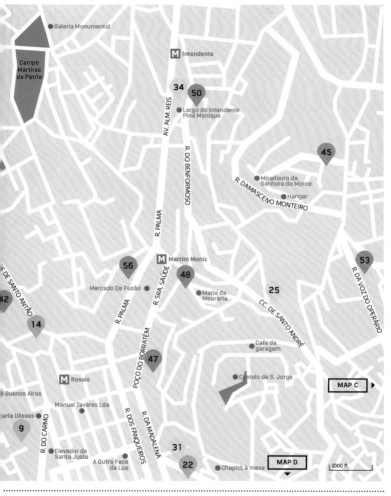

- Galeria Monumental
- Campo Mártires da Pátria
- **M** Intendente
- **34** **50** Largo do Intendente Pina Manique
- AV. ALM. REIS
- R. DO BENFORMOSO
- **45**
- Miradouro da Senhora do Monte
- R. DAMASCENO MONTEIRO
- Hangar
- R. PALMA
- **56**
- **M** Martim Moniz
- **48**
- R. SRA. SAÚDE
- Mercado De Fusão
- Maria da Mouraria
- **25**
- CC. DE SANTO ANDRÉ
- R. DA VOZ DO OPERÁRIO
- **53**
- DE SANTO ANTÃO
- **42**
- **14**
- R. PALMA
- POÇO DO BORRATÉM
- Café da garagem
- **47**
- **M** Rossio
- Castelo de S. Jorge
- **MAP C** ▶
- Buenos Aires
- Manuel Tavares Lda
- aria Ulisses
- **9**
- R. DO CARMO
- R. DOS FANQUEIROS
- R. DA MADALENA
- Elevador de Santa Justa
- A Outra Face da Lua
- **31**
- **22**
- Chapitó à mesa
- **MAP D** ▼
- 1000 ft.

105

DISTRICT MAP : **BAIRRO ALTO, CHIADO, CAIS DO SODRÉ**

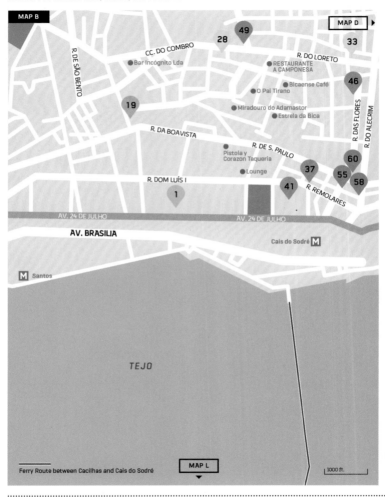

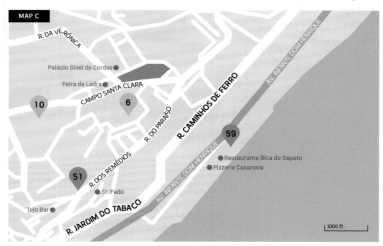

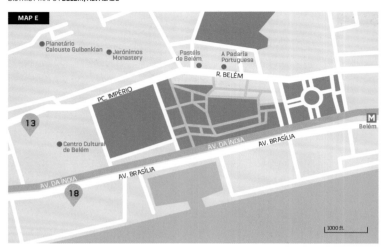

- 13_Museu Coleção Berardo
- 16_Appleton Square
- 18_Espaço Espelho d'Água
- 20_Galeria Vera Cortês

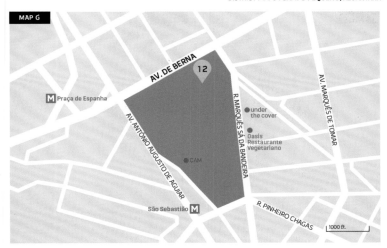

MAP G

AV. DE BERNA

12

Praça de Espanha

R. MARQUÊS SÁ DA BANDEIRA

AV. MARQUÊS DE TOMAR

AV. ANTÓNIO AUGUSTO DE AGUIAR

under the cover

Oasis Restaurante Vegetariano

CAM

São Sebastião

R. PINHEIRO CHAGAS

1000 ft.

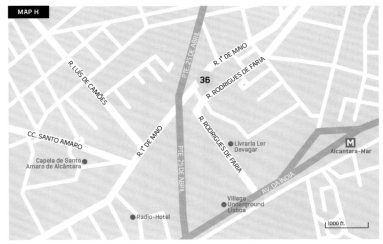

MAP H

R. LUÍS DE CAMÕES

PTE. 25 DE ABRIL

R. 1º DE MAIO

R. RODRIGUES DE FARIA

36

CC. SANTO AMARO

R. 1º DE MAIO

PTE. 25 DE ABRIL

R. RODRIGUES DE FARIA

Livraria Ler Devagar

Alcântara-Mar

Capela de Santo Amaro de Alcântara

AV. DA ÍNDIA

Village Underground Lisboa

Radio-Hotel

1000 ft.

- 12_Fundação Calouste Gulbenkian
- 36_LX Factory

DISTRICT MAPS : **MARVILA, BENFICA, ALCÂNTARA, ALMADA**

MAP I

MAP J

MAP K

MAP L

- ● 2_Elevador da Boca do Vento
- ● 7_Panorâmico de Monsanto
- ● 17_Museu Nacional de Etnologia
- ● 21_Underdogs Gallery

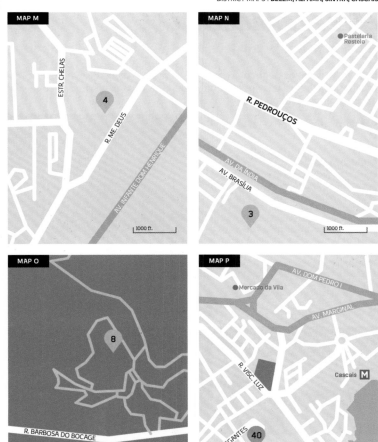

- 3_Centro Champalimaud
- 4_Museu Nacional do Azulejo
- 8_Sintra
- 40_Pizzeria–il Siciliano

Accommodation

Hip hostels, fully-equipped apartments & swanky hotels

No journey is perfect without a good night's sleep to recharge. Whether you're backpacking or on a business trip, our picks combine top quality and convenience, whatever your budget.

 <€80   €81–200   >€201+

Areias do Seixo

The modern architecture of Areias do Seixo is an angular concrete and glass fantasy contrasted by their sustainable, earth-loving ideology. Visitors can choose between four types of equally luxurious rooms, each with a distinct flavour. The boutique hotel has a vegetable garden which visitors can volunteer to help with in preparation for dinner. Alternatively, visitors can enjoy a 5 minute walk to the beach and relax before the seaside.

🏠 *Povoa de Penafirme, 2560–046*
📞 *+351 261 936 340*
URL *www.areiasdoseixo.com*

The Independente Hostel & Suites

The Art Deco–inspired Independente Hostel and Suites is either classically elegant or strikingly trendy depending on whether visitors choose the vintage boho-chic suites or bold triple-bunk hostel beds. Immerse in an atmosphere in between classy and laid-back at the Decadente. Some rooms have balconies with river views.

🏠 *R. São Pedro de Alcântara 81, 1250–238*
📞 *+351 213 461 381* 🔗 *theindependente.pt*

Memmo Alfama

Located in the quaint Alfama district, Memmo Alfama integrates itself within the Portuguese capital with its pure and minimal room designs so that the surroundings may speak for themselves. Indulge in the breakfast buffet, and later on the rich history of the picturesque buildings and monuments, right in its surroundings.

🏠 Tv. Merceeiras 27, 1100–348
📞 +351 21 049 5660
URL www.memmohotels.com/alfama

Baixa House

🏠 R. dos Fanqueiros 81, 1100-227
📞 +351 91 909 0895
🌐 www.baixahouse.com/en

Palácio Belmonte

🏠 Páteo Dom Fradique 14, 1100-624
📞 +351 21 881 6600
🌐 palaciobelmonte.com

Casas NaAreia

🏠 Sítio da Carrasqueira, 7580-613, Comporta
📞 +351 93 441 8316
🌐 casasnaareia.com

Notes

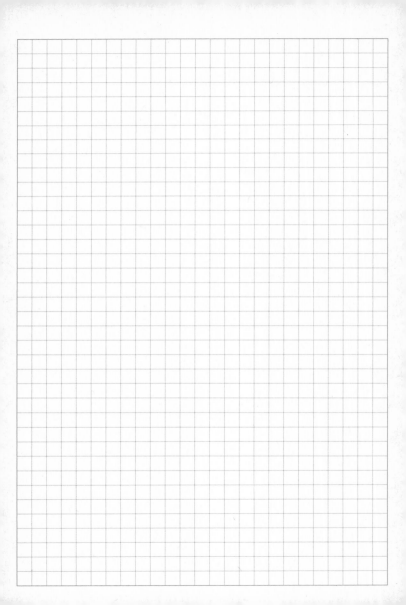

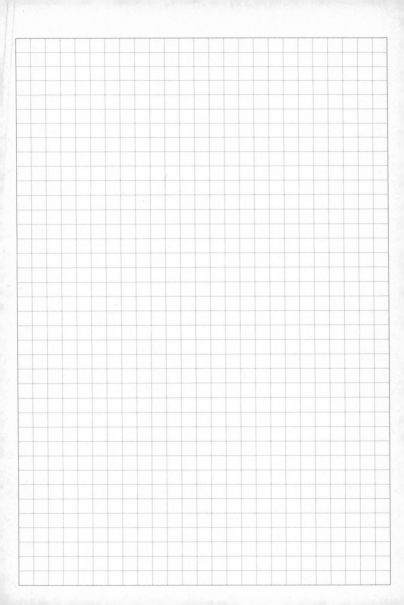

Index

In Accommodation: all courtesy of respective hotels. Baxia House, by Ana Carvalho. CasasNaAreia, by Nelson Garrido.

CITIX60

CITIx60: Lisbon

First published and distributed by
viction workshop ltd

viction:ary™

7C Seabright Plaza, 9-23 Shell Street,
North Point, Hong Kong

Url: www.victionary.com
Email: we@victionary.com
🅵 @victionworkshop
🅥 @victionary_
🅘 @victionworkshop

Edited and produced by viction:ary

Concept & art direction: Victor Cheung
Research & editorial: Queenie Ho, Caroline Kong
Project coordination: Elisabeth Kwan, Jovan Lip, Katherine Wong
Design & map illustration: MW Wong, Frank Lo

Contributing curator & coordinator: Pedro Lopes Pereira
Contributing writer: Monique Todd
Cover map illustration: Angela aka Kruella
Count to 10 illustrations: Guillaume Kashima aka Funny Fun
Photography: Francisco Nogueira, José Sarmento de Matos

Content is compiled based on facts available as of March 2017. Travellers are
advised to check for updates from respective locations before your visit.

First edition
ISBN 978-988-13204-1-4
Printed and bound in China

Acknowledgements

A special thank you to all creatives, photographer(s), editor, producers, com-
panies and organisations for your crucial contributions to our inspiration and
knowledge necessary for the creation of this book. And, to the many whose
names are not credited but have participated in the completion of the book,
we thank you for your input and continuous support all along.